MEN
MAMMALS
AND
MORALS

MEN MAMMALS AND MORALS

SHIV DHAWAN

PARTRIDGE
A Penguin Random House Company

ISBN: Hardcover   978-1-4828-2319-6
             Softcover   978-1-4828-2321-9
             eBook   978-1-4828-2320-2

To order additional copies of this book, contact
Partridge India
000 800 10062 62
orders.india@partridgepublishing.com

www.partridgepublishing.com/india

CONTENTS

Dedicated to:

Saraswati
Goddess of Learning,
May this work please Her in many hearts.

Also dedicated to my family, father late Jagdish Dhawan a prince amongst men, my mother Gajinder Dhawan, my wife Sareena and my two children Madhav and Chandni

ACKNOWLEDGEMENTS

As a seven year old child I chanced upon a copy of Arthur Ryder's translation of the Panchatantra and requested my mother to read out a story every morning at the breakfast table. Those early impressions remained with me throughout the years and in 1975 I decided to render some of my favourite fables into verse. The result is before the reader.

Here I would be failing in imparting my debt of gratitude to my preceptors and gurus if I do not express my indebtedness to the great scholar Vishnusharman, without whom none of us would ever have had the opportunity to receive such ideas as are contained in the Panchatantra.

Words cannot express my gratitude to my late father Jagdish Dhawan, who painstakingly drew all the sketches for this book, proving that besides his all-round expertise, he was a brilliant but shy artist.

I am also grateful to K. Ramakrishnan, Editor of the Children's World for publishing the following poems in his magazine-Brain Drain, Blue Jackal, The Talking Cave, Brahmin's Goat, Supersmart, Golden Voice, Foolish Friend, Numbskull, The Brahmin & Thief and the Ghost.

There no more fitting preface to a collection of poems than yet another verse. Whenever I have sought the opinion of the world at large on lines penned during a pensive mood, I have been asked one fundamental question,' Why did you write these poems?' Like the famous mountaineer who on being asked why he had scaled Mount Everest replied very matter of factly, 'Because it was there!' I too could say I wrote them because I simply had to. However the truth is that

Whenever my soul grows weary of worldly miseries, it sheds tears of blood, which on drying become poetry!

I would like to record my sincere appreciation for Joginder Goswami from the Library of Delhi Gymkhana club for painstakingly and accurately typing all the poems in record time. My wife Sareena daughter Chandni and my mother Gajinder Dhawan I thank over and over again for patiently hearing me recite different draft versions of each poem. I am grateful to my son Madhav for reworking on the illustrations and formatting. Numerous friends too have calmly been through the torture of reading the poems and then hearing my diatribes. There are too many to acknowledge in person but to all I express my gratitude. Nothing motivates a poet more than an appreciative audience.

C 1/34 Safdarjung Development Area,
New Delhi—110016

SHIV DHAWAN—A PROFILE

Born in Kolkata (West Bengal) on 25th November 1961, Shiv had a brilliant academic career. Graduating first class first in Philosophy (Honours) from St. Stephen's College, University of Delhi in 1983 he won the Indian Philosophical Congress Gold Medal and was awarded the All India Post Graduate Scholarship by the University of Delhi for two years. He passed first class first Master of Arts in Philosophy from Hindu College (University of Delhi) in 1985 winning his second gold medal from the Indian Philosophical Congress along with the N. V. Thadani Memorial Prize. In 1986, Shiv Dhawan secured first class first in M. Phil (part I) setting a new record in Indian Philosophy and aggregate marks. He was granted the University Grants Commission Research Fellowship for four years and direct admission to Ph. D. in the Department of Philosophy, University of Delhi.

Early in his scholastic days, Shiv displayed a flair for 'communication' which he persistently developed over hundreds of published articles, reviews, stories, philosophical poems and research papers. He was founder Secretary of Association of Writers and Illustrators for Children, New Delhi, 1981-82; Guest Lecturer in Philosophy at Hindu College 1985-86. He has been a management

SHIV DHAWAN

consultant for last twenty five years working in the sphere of organization and people transformation in India, China, Bhutan, Sultanate of Oman, Canada and the USA. He presently works as a Strategic Management Advisor to several organisations.

Shiv lives in New Delhi with his mother, wife who is a school teacher and two children. Besides writing, he loves collecting antique wrist watches and listening to classical music and unwinding through swimming in the Delhi Gymkhana Club of which he is a second generation permanent member. He also enjoys travelling to far off places with a particular interest in wildlife parks, places of historical importance and hill resorts.

INTRODUCTION

The Panchatantra (The five tantras or books of knowledge) is a perennial source of wisdom, which has been read throughout the length and breadth of the civilized world. Translations and adaptations of this work are found in almost all the principal languages of the world.

In terms of historicity, these fables have been current in the Indian socio-cultural ethos for thousands of years. Their popularity can be gauged from the fact that currently over two hundred different versions exist spread over more than fifty languages.

The original collection of the Panchatantra stories, written in Sanskrit, numbered eighty four. But in their endless travel through the ages these fascinating stories metamorphosed not only with respect to the form, colour and setting, but even in their total number.

DATE

The exact place of origin and time of the Panchatantra is a matter of great controversy. Scholars like Dr. Hertel claim that it was composed in Kashmir, about 200 B.C., while others feel that the period between 1200 B.C. to 300 B.C.

would be a safer guess. The first literal and faithful translation of the Panchatantra into a European language was Theodor Benfry's German translation of 1859, which oriental scholars regard as the most authoritative version in existence.

Subsequently Stanley Rice (1924) and Franklin Edgarton (1924) ('The Panchatantra Reconstructed') a professor of Sanskrit, at the University of Pennsylvania, and Arthur Ryder proved to be popular translators of this text.

NATURE, STYLE AND CONTENTS

Instead of delineating the chronology of the Panchatantra, something which many litterateurs have already done, I would like to delve into some of its merits to explore what the Panchatantra really is. Literature of whatever kind it be, cannot be isolated from the life of the people. The Panchatantra is therefore regarded as a 'Niti-shastra' where 'Niti' could be understood to mean the right conduct or wise conduct. Although there is no English equivalent for the term 'Niti' it could be safely compared to Aristotle's concept of 'Practical Wisdom' as explained in the Nichomachaen Ethics. To quote Ryder "Niti . . . . the harmonious development of the powers of man, a life in which security, prosperity, resolute action friendship, and good learning are so combined as to produce joy. It is a noble ideal, shaming many tawdry ambitions, many vulgar catch words of our day . . . ."

Aristotle defined 'Practical' Wisdom' as the practice and habit of deliberating well. It is a habit of correctly sizing up a situation, of evaluating the problem at hand in terms of its general characteristics and then of deciding the way it is to be handled and the time it is to be done, keeping in mind the welfare of the individual as a whole. The Panchatantra therefore gives us in a capsule form the broad principles which ought to regulate our conduct in society, ensuring that the human species as a whole thrives.

The origin of this book of fables is enshrined in a particularly endearing fable. It is held that once upon a time there reigned a mighty monarch named Immortal Power, who had three sons all of whom were blockheads of the first order. The King sought the aid of many men of letters as tutors for the princes, but to no avail. Finally when he was sick to the teeth with his three dunces there came to his court a Brahmin named Vishnusharman who assured the dejected monarch that within six months he would convert the indolent princes into incomparable masters of the numerous sciences or else forfeit his life.

The King at his wits end, saw a ray of hope and instructed his sons to accompany the Brahmin to the latter's ashrama to try and imbibe whatever he taught them. Thinking the trip to be a new game, the princes gaily followed Vishnusharman.

Knowing their aversion to the staid classroom atmosphere, Vishnusharman resorted to a sort of non-formal education by telling the princes stories and asking them what moral each fable conveyed. Ensconced in sylvan surroundings the princes gradually came to realize that thinking was not such a boring occupation after all. Their thirst for knowledge was enkindled, and they requested Vishnusharman to instruct them in other sciences as also in statecraft. After the stipulated six months when the trio returned to the palace, the King joyfully noted a strange glow on their faces, his sons were no longer blockheads . . . . Vishnusharman's fables had achieved the impossible.

These fables of Vishnusharman were subsequently collected and presented as a treatise called the 'Panchatantra'. As the name suggests, this work is divided into five books entitled —

I.   The Loss of Friends
II. The Winning of Friends
III. Crows and Owls
IV. Loss of Gains
V.   Ill Considered Action

Most of the characters in Vishnusharman's fables are animals which have a fairly constant character.

Thus for instance, the lion is usually depicted as a stupid fellow, while the jackal is always shown to be cunning, outwitting his adversaries with consummate ease. Each of the five books is independent of the others and consists of a main framing story, and numerous secondary stories related as appropriate occasions permit.

THE BLUE JACKAL

A jackal named Fierce Howl
in a city for food began to prowl.
On seeing him the dogs began to snap and bite
thus putting the poor jackal to flight.

The curs chased him into an indigo vat
where now all blue in colour, he sadly sat.
Destined by Nature to survive
he climbed out and into the forest arrived.

Deciding to take advantage of his state
he made other creatures feel that he was great.
Some animals scared, were prepared to vamoose,
while still others on seeing him let all hell loose.

Fierce Howl bossed over everyone, small and big
all were subservient, right from the lion down to the pig.
He made his brother jackals do all sorts odd things,
and behaved like a tyrant—king of kings.

One day a pack of jackals began to moan,
hearing which, Fierce Howl replied in a shrill tone.
On hearing his howls the animals' anger grew,
and surrounding him they gave him his just due.

Hence, whoever corrupt power begins to cherish,
like the foolish jackal will soon perish.

THE BRAHMIN'S GOAT

Three hungry rogues seeing a Brahmin carrying a goat
thought to themselves—a man to thrive must needs keep alive.
They also knew, that where flattery fails
intrigue is most certain to avail.

Disguising themselves according to a plan
one by one they approached the saintly man.
"Oh holy sir carrying a pig is a sin".
"You are a fool Sir!" the Brahmin began to yell
"As between a goat and a pig the difference you cannot tell".

Then the second rogue asked why he carried a dead calf,
adding, "Touch not anything which lifeless lies
as such a sin not even a Yagna purifies".
The holy man let out a sarcastic laugh
calling him a fool for mistaking a goat for a calf.

The third enquired why he lugged a donkey
it was inauspicious and misfortune was sure.
Scared by now he hastened to the Ganges pure
handing over his prized goat to the third man
who, with the others carried out their crafty plan.

THE MEDDLESOME MONKEY

On the outskirts of a forest was a city
where a temple was being built.
Every day, at noon when the sun was high,
craftsmen stopping work, would sit and rest nearby.

One day, during the rest hour,
a troop of monkeys entered the grounds.
They began to play and romp about,
often in sheer joy, they would scream and shout.

Then, a monkey whose end (it seems) was near,
sat upon a log with a wedge in it.
Exclaimed the curious monkey, "My it is indeed queer,
for someone to stick a wooden peg here".

With that, he set about the arduous task
of pulling loose the wedge.
which emerged just where his private parts entered the cleft . . . .
what happen thereafter, to your imagination is left.

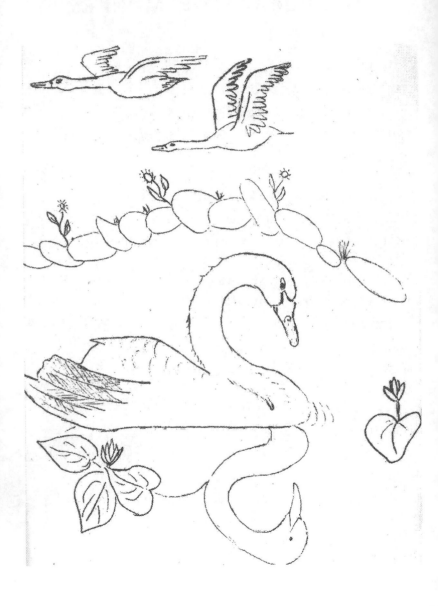

THE UNSOCIAL SWANS

There lived a king named Gay Chariot
who owned a serenely swaying lotus lake.
Enhancing its beauty, were golden swans who lived thither
paying a half yearly rent of one tail feather.

Once a great golden bird came
seeking solace to this lake.
But the residents protested, "You cannot stay,
this lake is ours, just go away."

This led to heated argument,
the newcomer sent an appeal to the king.
Hearing the entire episode, the Monarch grew so vexed
he ordered his men to cut off the swans' necks.

Now, one old bird seeing soldiers coming armed,
warned his feathered mates.
Who unanimously decided to fly away . . . .
so they could live to see another day.

Therefore be generous in receiving the needy guest,
or else face the fate of the swans from the lotus nest.

THE TALKING CAVE

A hungry lion named Rough Claw
while foraging in the forest a cave saw.
To which some creature would return at night
and thus provide him with a tasty bite.

Presently—a jackal named Curd Face came about
and saw pug marks going in his cave,
but none coming out.
To validate his fears a clever trick he did try,
he called out to the cave and waited for a reply.

He yelled out a greeting to the cave,
the lion thinking the cave spoke, a roar in reply
gave.
Curd Face thought, in all the forests he had walked,
never had he come across a cave that talked!

Realizing Rough Claw's crafty plan,
the jackal, laughing at the lion's foolishness,
ran . . . .

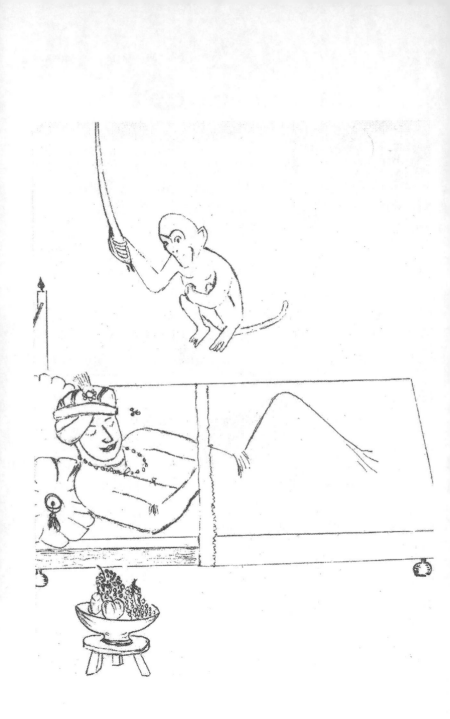

THE FOOLISH FRIEND

A king for his sword bearer had a monkey
who was very devoted to his master.
Compared to courtiers, in everything he was faster.
He spent his time swimming in the palace moat,
often he would plague the ministers in court.
Still of his ape the king was very fond,
and each passing day strengthened this friendship
bond.
One day, as the king in his garden lay,
to serve his master the monkey decided to stay.
Presently a bee came and sat on the monkey's arm.
While the primate was thinking of how to do it harm
it flew and hovered over the king, and
as the ape tried to get rid of it with a wave of the
hand,
it buzzed and escaped, which was not surprising,
though the monkey's temper was now rising.
Now, when the little bee sat on the Monarch's
head . . . .
the monkey lifted a sword-the next moment the king
was dead.

THE MONKEY'S FIRE

In a certain part of a forest
a band of monkey's found a firefly.
They lifted the 'Fire' with great care
and carried it back to their lair.

Covering it with dry leaves and grass
they thrust forward their bodies to enjoy the warmth.
One of the monkeys, feeling cold, began to blow,
but the firefly continued to just glow.

Just then a bird sitting above chirruped,
there was no fire to be blown at, it was a mere fly.
The monkey to her wise counsel paid no heed
and carried on with his fire blowing deed.

But the bird was really persistent
and began screaming into the monkey's ear.
The now infuriated monkey seizing the bird's head,
pitched her against a rock-dead.

Thus, just as no man can bend the unrelenting tree,
similarly, no good advice had ever helped imbecility.

THE LION AND THE RAM

In a dense forest lived a ram
who had become separated from his flock.
In his armour of fleece and horns, he roamed the woods
trying to look as formidable as he could.

Once, while wandering in the jungle
he came across a huge hungry lion.
Seeing the ram's menacing horns and bristling hair
the king of beasts got a terrible scare.

Another day, the hungry lion saw the ram
nibbling grass in a shady glade,
and thought, "Since on mere greenery he does dine,
this creature obviously is a prey of mine".

So, without further ado,
he pounced and killed the unsuspecting ram.
Thus, the weak are always in dire need
of keeping secret on what they feed.

THE GREEDY JACKAL

There was a herd of docile sheep
grazing in an open field.
Suddenly two rams began using horns and heads
in a desperate bid to tear each other to shreds.

They would angrily draw apart and charge again,
head crashing, and rivulets of blood flowing.
Presently, a hungry jackal was attracted to the scene
where, he began to lick the blood drops clean.

Being obviously a dull witted creature
he yielded to the temptation of greed.
Hoping to have a greater feast,
he advanced between the grappling beasts.

But then what happened to our friend
when the rams charged just where he stood . . . .
The jackal caught between the crashing heads
sailed through the air, hitting the ground-dead.

Thus the jackal, the glutton that he was,
died because he could not control his jaws.

GOLDEN VOICE

There was a dhobi called Clean Cloth
who fodder for his starving donkey sought.
Due to lack of food the animal was getting thin
even the ribs showed beneath his skin.

On his way a tiger skin he did see
and to himself mused he,
if the donkey dressed in the skin was left to graze at
night,
the farmers would not harm it out of fright.

The next night according to plan,
the 'dressed' donkey was left in a barley field by the
man.
That night a mare close by did neigh,
the donkey in reply, began to bray.

The farmers seeing through the trick,
belaboured the donkey with stones and many a stick.

Although in tiger skin he was arrayed,
the donkey was killed-because he brayed.

LOUSY DEATH

On the very bed where a mighty monarch did sleep
lived with her family, a female louse named Creep.

On blue blood alone she and her children did feed,
the bed seemed to fulfil all their material needs.

Presently a flea named Leap, saw the king one night,
and eagerly landed to have many a juicy bite.

Creep warned him to stop, but Leap wanted one
more nip,
after all, it was not everywhere that he got royal
blood to sip.

Feeling a sting, the king ordered his men to hunt out
the pest,
and destroy it forthwith, along with its entire nest.

Having had his fill, Leap out of the room did crawl,
while soldiers, upon finding Creep and family, killed
them all.

Hence with no stranger share your house,
or else, you may meet with the fate of Creep the
louse.

THE DOG WHO WENT ABROAD

In a certain town afflicted by a famine,
a dog named Spot from lack of food was getting thin.
In a bid to find a place to eat in and stay
he set off for another city far away.

This city had a house where eatables were carelessly kept
into which, our friend Spot now crept.
Here, he ate his fill from a diversified bill of fare,
everyday returning for all his meals there.

Once, when he was returning after licking the platter clean,
other pariah dogs, drunk with aristocratic spleen,
closing in on him, attacked poor Spot,
on the road one of the worst canine battles was fought.

Managing to escape, Spot thought, "Better one's own home,
where, even in times of famine one can peacefully roam".
After having thought things over and devised an escape plan,
back to his own famine stricken city Spot the dog ran.

At home, relatives often asked about the foreign place,
and the various difficulties he had to face.
Spot replied "The food is good, and does not lack variety
but kinsmen in that foreign street are lacking in sobriety".

THE THREE FISHES

In a lake where fish did abound,
three fish-Forethought, Readywit and Fatalist were
found.
One day, Forethought heard some fishermen say,
that they would fish in that lake the next day.

He thought, "If they return here,
our death will surely be near.
So, I will take my friends and flee
far away to some other water body".

Readywit said, "I'm invincible, nobody can strike
me dead
since I can protect myself by using my head.
So, here in the abode of my ancestors I shall stay,
if you so wish, the two of you can go away".

Said Fatalist, "I too won't leave the place where I
was born
just because some fishermen are coming the next
morn".
Sadly Forethought bid a final goodbye to his mates,
and set off upstream, leaving them to their fates.

The fishermen came, just as the fish had thought,
and Readywit along with Fatalist in their nets were
caught.
Readywit pretended to be already dead when put in
a sack,
and luckily into the water was thrown back.

But Fatalist, instead of wisely playing dead,
struggled hard, and was repeatedly clubbed on the
head.
Thus Forethought and Readywit somehow managed
to thrive,
while Fatalist, the dim witted, couldn't even remain
alive.

THE BRAHMIN'S DREAM

Seedy a Brahmin, being very poor,
lived by begging from door to door.
Once, getting some barley from afar,
he hung it from the ceiling in a jar.

Lying on the cot and staring at the jar,
he fell into a hypnotic reverie.
If a famine were to occur, thought he,
I will sell the barley and get some money,

With that money I will buy a pair of goats . . . .
thus the Brahmin began to gloat.
In a year their numbers will rise,
which in turn will fetch a good price.

With that money I'll have cows there,
why! I will even have a horse and a mare
Then, some of the creatures will be sold
thus bringing me more and more gold.

Afterwards a mansion I shall make,
but where? Why not by the side of the lake?
Then, I will wed a pretty damsel and have a boy,
playing with whom will give me utmost joy.

SHIV DHAWAN

But when the boy disregards me
and makes me angry,
when, of his childish jokes I grow sick,
I shall rise and give him a hard kick.

I will kick him like this . . . . See . . . . ,
and in his hypnotic reverie,
the Brahmin kicked out too far . . . . ,
his foot struck and broke the barley filled jar.

Hence if you indulge in hopes which are too high
like Seedy, shattered your fantasies will lie.

THE MONKEY'S HEART

On the bank of a river,
Red Face, the monkey lived on an apple tree.
Laden with fruit all the year around,
the tree kept the primate's health sound.

Perchance a crocodile named Ugly Mug came, and
getting out of thc water, basked on the shore.
Accepting him as his friends and guest,
Red Face gave him fruit at his behest.

At home, Ugly Mug bragged of the land where fruits
abound
and of the monkey friends he had made.
His wife, being consumed with jealousy
plotted to kill this monkey.

She requested him to present her the monkey's heart
causing Ugly Mug to jump up with a start.
He tried to reason out with his wife,
who said if he refused, she would take her life.

To get away from his wife's angry taunts
he set off for Red Face's tree.
He implored that his wife wished to see him some day
to which Red Face agreed, and they set off right away.

He sat on Ugly Mug's back, who, on reaching the middle
began to submerge, causing Red Face to let out a scream.
Here, the croc . . . . thinking himself to be very smart,
growled, "Now I will give my wife your heart".

The monkey thought and he thought, and he thought
the more he thought, the more scared he got.
His whole body was trembling with fear
as no ways and means of saving his neck were clear.

Suddenly he began prancing with glee,
exclaiming that his heart was left behind on the tree.
The crocodile vexed at not being told at the start,
turned back to enable Red Face to collect his heart.

On nearing the shore, the monkey leapt off the back
thanking the Gods for getting him home safely.
Then turning to Ugly Mug he ordered him to depart
saying, that none could survive without a heart.

Thus with the help of resourcefulness and guile
Red Face saved himself from the crocodile.

THE HERON'S MEAL

An old heron living by the side of a pond
of eating fish was very fond.
One day, he devised an easy way of catching fish
and eating them with relish.

He began lingering by the pond side
and often, while sitting cried.
A crab enquired, "Why are you so blue?"
He replied, "Because misfortune is to befall you".

The fish cried out in unison, "Uncle save us".
and began to make a terrible fuss.
The crafty bird said word had come from God,
that at dawn a man was coming with a fishing rod.

The inhabitants begged him to save them all
and his good qualities they began to extol.
They pleaded that since he knew of the calamity,
he also must be having some remedy.

The heron said they could be flown to a lake
where everyone a new home could make.
All the fish, considering the bird to be a friend,
agreed to follow to the very end.

The fish were taken one by one in his beak
up to a high and barren rocky peak.
There, the heron gobbled up all the fish he could eat,
and for some time thrived on the meat.

A crab sensed that something was amiss
as there was no news from the transported fish.
He implored the bird to take him to the lake,
as he wished to see it—just for satisfaction's sake

The heron taking him on his back for a ride
showed the peak of death with pride.
Thought the wise crab, "When an awesome
apparition appears,
strike, and set aside your fears".

Acting fast, he bit off the heron's head
causing it to drop to earth—dead.
Thus, the heron whose greed was never satisfied,
fell prey to a mere crab, and died.

BRAIN DRAIN

Once a lion that was very old
retained a jackal for a servant, I'm told.
Who was very loyal to his master
and being younger could run much faster.
Bringing his Majesty a kill each day
he kept the lion's hunger pangs at bay.

One day, a plump ass the lion espied,
"I must have it for dinner!" he cried.
The jackal set off his master's meal to book
and nab the ass by hook or by crook.

Greeting the creature, he praised him a lot,
extolling the virtues he just hadn't got.
Inducing the fool to walk into the den
he revelled in his treachery—a real number ten.

On seeing his meal the lion pounced, hastily,
but the ass darted off reaching home safety.
The jackal was cross with the lion for being rash,
his brilliant scheme had been so clumsily smashed.

Returning to the ass he said, "Why all the fuss
when his Lordship only desired to make you one of us"?
The simpleton agreed to go back to the lair
and was killed by the lion . . . . then and there.

The lion then went to bathe, leaving his attendant on
guard.
The jackal thought and thought real hard,
that the lion was glutton indeed,
once he began eating, nothing would remain on
which to feed.

So without further refrain,
The canny jackal ate up the ass's brain.
When the lion came back,
he saw that the ass's head sported a big crack.

Angrily he enquired about the whereabouts of the
brain,
the jackal replied, "Sire, if he had any, would he
have come again?"

THE FEET WASHING FIEND

In a forest Cruel the fiend, had his retreat,
where every passing Brahmin he would eat.
One day climbing onto a wandering brahmin's head
"I'm going to eat you up", he said.

The hapless Brahmin getting a terrible fright
began praying for deliverance from his plight,
suddenly he saw Cruel's feet were soft like lotus
hearts
and looked incongruous, compared to his other
parts.

"You look awful", the Brahmin gasped, "but have
beautiful feet—how?"
"For", "replied Cruel, "Never to walk with
unwashed feet I have vowed".
Hearing this, the Brahmin couldn't help feeling
mighty glad
as now a way of saving himself through duping the
fiend he had.

Presently the duo came to a lake
where the fiend announced, "Before dinner, a bath I
always take".
Telling the Brahmin to remain rooted to the spot
into the water Cruel the fiend got.

The Brahmin knew his life depended on his acting
fast
if the fiend returned, these moments could well be
his last.
He knew that Cruel would not compete,
in running with the Brahmin, especially with
unwashed feet.

He watched, intently, noticing Cruel inattentive at
one stage.
the Brahmin sprinted away, leaving the fiend
seething with rage.
Hence a wise man is he who observes facts, not
always plain
just as the Brahmin once caught by the fiend, got
away again.

NUMSKULL

A lion named Numskull drunk with pride
used to kill and eat any animal he spied.
Soon, as all the animals began to die,
reasoning with the lion they wanted to try.

Begging him to stop the sinful thing as killing
subjects did not befit a king.
They promised each day to send him a beast
on which the lion could freely feast.

Hearing them Numskull readily agreed,
that what he had done was a terrible deed.
But he added, if an animal did not come each day,
then again on all the animals he would prey.

Hence every day he got some animal for dinner,
while the forest population grew thinner.
Once, it being All Rabbits Day,
a little rabbit set out on his way.

He got an idea by which the lion he could kill
and come back home, alive still.
So to while away time, he began to go slow
and, upon reaching the lion late, bowed low.

Numskull's soul with anger was flaming,
for the delay the animals he was blaming.
Seeing a puny tardy rabbit, his meal, at the door,
he let out a loud and angry roar.

Pretending to tremble with fright
the rabbit told the lion of his plight.
He said that another lion wanting to sup-had tried
to attack and eat him up.

Not only that, he had called Numskull a thief,
adding that he was a totally false chief.
Numskull with blazing mien
asked the rabbit to take him to the rude lion.

The rabbit, in a well to Numskull his image did show,
which, when he roared replied with an echo.
Jumping into the well, to attack his image he tried
and thus the foolish Numskull died.

Hence intelligence is power, but nowhere

can power and foolishness make a lasting pair.

SUPERSMART

A jackal named Supersmart who in a forest did stay
came across a dead elephant one day.
He knew that the elephant's skin was tough,
to bite through which, his own teeth were not enough.

Then, on spying a lion, he hit upon a plan,
Saluting the royal creature
he told him the elephant he should eat,
while allowing his humble servant to press his feet.

The lion touched by the jackal's humility,
said that he did not eat anything killed by another,
instead, he graciously bestowed it upon the crafty beast
who began to have visions of a big feast.

Presently a tiger came around
and began to eye the pachyderm longingly,
Just then Supersmart began to shout,
"Run uncle run, there is a lion about".

The tiger with tail between his legs slunk away
after begging Supersmart not to speak about his presence.

The jackal gleefully thought, "Wherever a hero is found,
there exists a villain to knock him to the ground".

But still the hide was uncut,
and, as the jackal was growing hungrier
he saw a young leopard called Spot,
this caused his mind to hatch another cunning plot.

He told him the elephant had been killed by a lion,
adding that Spot could steal a meal,
while he, the jackal, would stand guard,
and on the lion's return would thump the ground
hard.

Spot had just cut the hide
when Supersmart began to thump,
causing him to abandon the carcass and flee
while the jackal looked at the elephant with glee.

Just then another jackal came on the scene
and tried in many ways to steal a bite.
But Supersmart seizing him by the mane,
made him seek the horizon, howling in pain.

Having got the hide cut

and done away with adversaries,
Supersmart sat down with a smile,
to enjoy elephant meat for a while.

THE LION MAKERS

Three scholarly Brahmins who were friends
set out on a long journey from their home town.
They decided to visit courts of different kings
where, using their wisdom they could win many
things.

With them was a fourth Brahmin
whom they collectively considered to be a fool.
He always seemed to have a dull air,
never knowing what was happening anywhere.

In the course of their travels
the four brahmins entered a dense forest.
There a skeleton of some animal they did see,
this caused them to jump with glee.

Here they thought, lies a golden chance
to test our prowess and skill.
"I will assemble the skeleton", sand the first man,
and set about implementing his plan.

"Now, I will add flesh and blood
to the skeleton", said the second Brahmin.
So saying, a miracle he did perform,
by giving the assembled skeleton an animate form.

Said the third man with glee,
"Now into this carcass I will breathe life".
To which the fourth Brahmin gave a reply,
"Brothers if that lion is brought to life you all will die".

"Be gone!" they cried aloud in unison,
"Do we not know where our good lies?"
"Then please give me a minute". Said he
and the fourth Brahmin swiftly climbed a tall tree.

True to his word, the third man gave the lion life,
who rose, roared, and pounced on the three.
After the reborn lion had gone elsewhere,
The surviving Brahmin climbing down, ran like a hare . . . .

NADUK AND THE BEAM

There lived a merchant named Naduk
who had lost his money.
Determined to make more,
he decided to set sail for far away shores.

In his house was an iron balance beam
which was passed down from his ancestors.
This, to merchant Lakshman he did pawn
and set off-on his travels at the break of dawn.

After many years of business and travel in foreign
lands
Naduk returned with twice as much money as
before.
When asking Lakshman for the beam, he even
offered the price,
but was told that it had been eaten up by mice.

Naduk, being a shrewd man, saw through the trick
and quickly devised a counter plan.
He said, "Lakshman, you are in no way to blame,
'tis my bad luck the beam was eaten up before I
came".

"I am going to the river for a bath".
declared Naduk,
"So please send your son to help in carrying my
things".
As Lakshman found it hard to say 'no',
he allowed his son to go.

On reaching the river bank,
Naduk shut the lad in a big cave and returned
wailing.
He told Lakshman that while going for walk
the boy had been carried off by a hawk.

Lakshman was furious at this deed
and threatened to take the matter to court.
Then Naduk confided that Lakshman his son could
meet
if he returned the beam which had been left for mice
to eat.

Lakshman dragged him to the city court
where Naduk was accused of carrying off the boy.
To this, he told the story of the beam, mice and the
walk,
not forgetting to add the part of the kidnapping
hawk.

Justice was meted out by the magistrates,
and, in the end everyone was happy it seems,
as Lakshman got back his boy, and Naduk his beam.

THE BRAHMIN,
THIEF AND THE GHOST

A poor Brahmin living in a certain place,
on alms alone life did face.
Once, out of pity someone gave him two calves,
which caused him to save his food by halves.

The calves which fulfilled the brahmin's need
caused a thief to be overcome with greed.
He thought, if the calves he could steal,
they would provide him with many a tasty meal.

So, taking some rope he set out one night
but on the way met a creature who gave him a fright.
The thief asking about his identity learnt,
a ghost named Truthful was he.

The thief said that he was cruel from within
as he was about to steal the calves of a poor
Brahmin.
Truthful who ate once every three days,
said he may,
consider eating the Brahmin that day.

Together they went to the Brahmin's dwelling
where, on who should attack first they began
quarrelling.
The ghost said that the cows would create such a
row
that the sleeping Brahmin would immediately know.

The thief said if the man were to wake before the
meal
then the calves he would not be able to steal.
In shrill angry tones they argued and spoke,
while, hearing the hubbub the Brahmin awoke.

The thief said, "This ghost will eat your now",
while Truthful said, "This fellow will steal you
cows".
In this manner they verbally fought,
while the Brahmin a method of escape sought.

On impulse he prayed to the deity he loved most,
thus ridding himself of the ghost.
Then lifting up a club after the thief he ran . . . .
saving his cows, and foiling the evil man's plan.

FRIENDS, FRIENDS, FRIENDS

In a certain city lived a man named Too Good
who everyday went into the forest to cut firewood.
In that forest a lion named Spotless did stay
with his retainers-a jackal and crow serving him all
day.

One day, while roaming the forest aimlessly,
Spotless came across Too Good cutting a tree,
Feeling lost, he approached the man and bowing
low,
of his desire to strike a friendship made a great
show.

"Friend lion", said the man, "always come alone to me,
as I feel I may not be able to face your family".
The lion agreed and gradually gave up hunting
beasts,
as on dainties served by Too Good he could feast.

His neglected retainers soon the pangs of hunger did
feel,
and asked the lion where he now are his meals.
Forgetting that about Too Good's food he should
keep mum,
he promised to take them along, so that they could
have some.

The next morn, Spotless with his companions trotted
up happily,
seeing them, the terrified Too Good quickly climbed
a tree.
The lion was amazed, "Friend come down, don't be
afraid",
but Too Good from his perch the lion did upbraid.

"Yours jackal doesn't reassure, your crow's sharp
bill offends,
You see me up a tree 'cause I don't like your
friends".

Nobody can ever in a king place any faith,
who to shabby attendants entrusts matters of state.

THE LEONINE JACKAL

In a dense jungle a lion and his wife,
to a pair of cubs gave life.
Each day the lion killed any animal he could find
on which, at night the whole family dined.

Once, after roaming in the jungle all day
and not finding any food coming his way,
he suddenly saw a baby jackal looking lost and
terrified.
and out of pity adopted it as the fifth member of his
pride.

His lioness considering the jackal to be very sweet,
gave it some food from the larder to eat.
After gobbling his meal, the jackal settled down
happily,
convinced, he was a member of the lion's family.

Along with the two cubs he spent his babyhood in
play
and romped through the forest the whole day.
Together the cubs and jackal would always prance
and feed,
never recognizing any difference in their breeds.

One day when the trio an elephant did see,
the cubs decided to pounce upon and kill the enemy.
"If he should strike us with his trunk" said the jackal pup,
"Then our days on earth would surely be up".

So, without saying anything further,
he ran and hid behind his foster mother.
Seeing their brother had from the warfield fearfully fled,
the two cubs also ran, afraid of being struck down dead.

At home, they told their mother of their flight
and how brother jackal was afraid of a fight.

The jackal, now getting very, very very angry,
said' I'm not scared, I can fight anybody".

The lioness then gently took him aside and lovingly said,
"You are intrepid and stout hearted, and in your head
you possess a scholar's analytic brain,
but my boy, in your family, no elephants are slain".

Then she told him that he was a jackal pup
"If my cubs realize this, they will eat you up".
Scared, the jackal ran away as fast as he could,
till he found other jackals deep in the woods.

THE PERT HEN SPARROW

Once during a cold February
a monkey took shelter under a tree.
Caught in a hailstorm, the slightest breeze,
caused him to almost freeze.

Seeing the plight of the shivering monkey,
a hen sparrow residing on a branch of the tree
said, "If you find the weather too cool,
why not build a house you fool"?

The monkey surprised, to himself said,
"Well, she really does possess a bloated head".
Besides, of self-conceit, all creatures have a good
supply,
just as a plover with its claws tries to prop the sky.

He roundly abused the interfering bird,
adding, that not another word should be heard.
But, the sparrow continued to ply him with advice,
saying that a house under the tree would look really nice.

Angry that a puny bird could act in a manner so brash,
the monkey climbing up the tree, her nest did smash.
Hence, those who give advice when the occasion is
not best
may meet the fate of the sparrow, which lost her nest.

THE SNAKE WHO PAID CASH

There was once a Brahmin in a certain place,
whose time was wholly spent in unproductive
farming.
He thought, "There must be some deity of the field,
who must be worshipped in order to get a good
yield".

Suddenly from behind an anthill rose a snake
which caused the Brahmin to reflect,
"Surely this must be the Lord of all the Land,
who if be honoured, will let my crops stand".

So saying, every day before starting his work
he would offer the snake a jar of milk.
But wonder of wonders, after emptying the jar,
before departing the snake would leave a gold dinar.

One day, the Brahmin having to go to the city
instructed his son to feed the friendly snake.
The lad not being satisfied with a dinar a day,
wanted to take them all, and take them right away.

So, next time the snake was drinking the milk,
he hit it on the head with a cudgel . . . .
Luckily the wary snake darted back, and was saved,
angered by treachery, it bit the boy, sending him to
his grave.

Departing he said, "Wealth may well be thrown
apart,
friendship, torn and patched again, lives in an aching
heart".

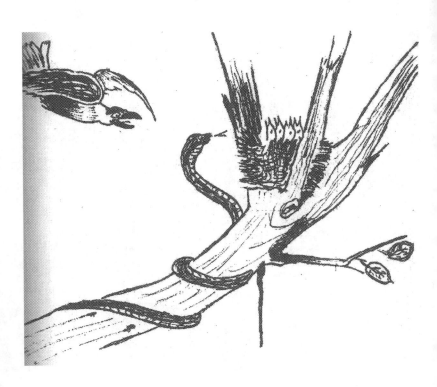

CHAIN REACTION

In a certain region grew a great banyan tree,
on which a crow and his wife lived happily.
One day, on the scene came a huge snake,
who a meal of the crow's eggs would make.

Even before the chicks were baptized,
the snake ate them right under their parents' eyes.
"Let us leave this tree", begged his wife,
but the crow wouldn't leave the place where he had
spent his life.

Said he, "By shrewd device I'll put an end to your
woes,
I'll bring death upon this villainous foe".
He and his jackal friend quickly a plan did make
of doing away with the vile snake.

As devised, the hen crow flew to a lake,
from where a bathing king's chain she did take.
She then headed straight for the snake's hole
followed by courtiers armed with sticks and poles.

Dropping the chain into the hole, gleefully,
she flew back to her chicks on the tree.
The snake emerged from within-raising his hissing head,
but the alert courtiers clubbed him down-dead.

Hence in places where brute force fails,
a shrewd and well thought plan may still prevail.
Just as the female crow used a golden chain,
with which the cruel snake was slain.

THE LAST TALK

A turtle named Shell Neck who lived in a lake,
with two ganders, Slim and Grim, friends did make.
Once, when a severe drought had caused the lake to
go dry,
to another water body the two ganders decided to
fly.

Having bid goodbye to Shell Neck, with a heavy
heart
they made preparations from their homestead to
depart.
But the turtle called out piteously to his friends
that without water he too would meet his end.

He then begged them that for friendship's sake,
they should take him along to the new lake.
The birds did not know what to do or say,
as they couldn't carry a turtle all the way.

Shell Neck said that he knew just the right
trick . . . . ,
the ganders could fly holding in their beaks a stick
which the turtle in turn would grip with his
teeth . . . .
My! wouldn't that be a marvellous flying feat!

"If Shell Neck were to open his mouth", said Slim,
"I'm sure that it would be the end of him".
To this the turtle gave a cheery reply,
"I promise not to talk once we are in the sky".

As they were passing over a town,
some people laughed, which caused the turtle to frown.
He foolishly opened his mouth to find out the joke
and plummeting down, died-all because he spoke.